MOTORCYCLE
RIDERS HUB

MODULE 2 COURSE

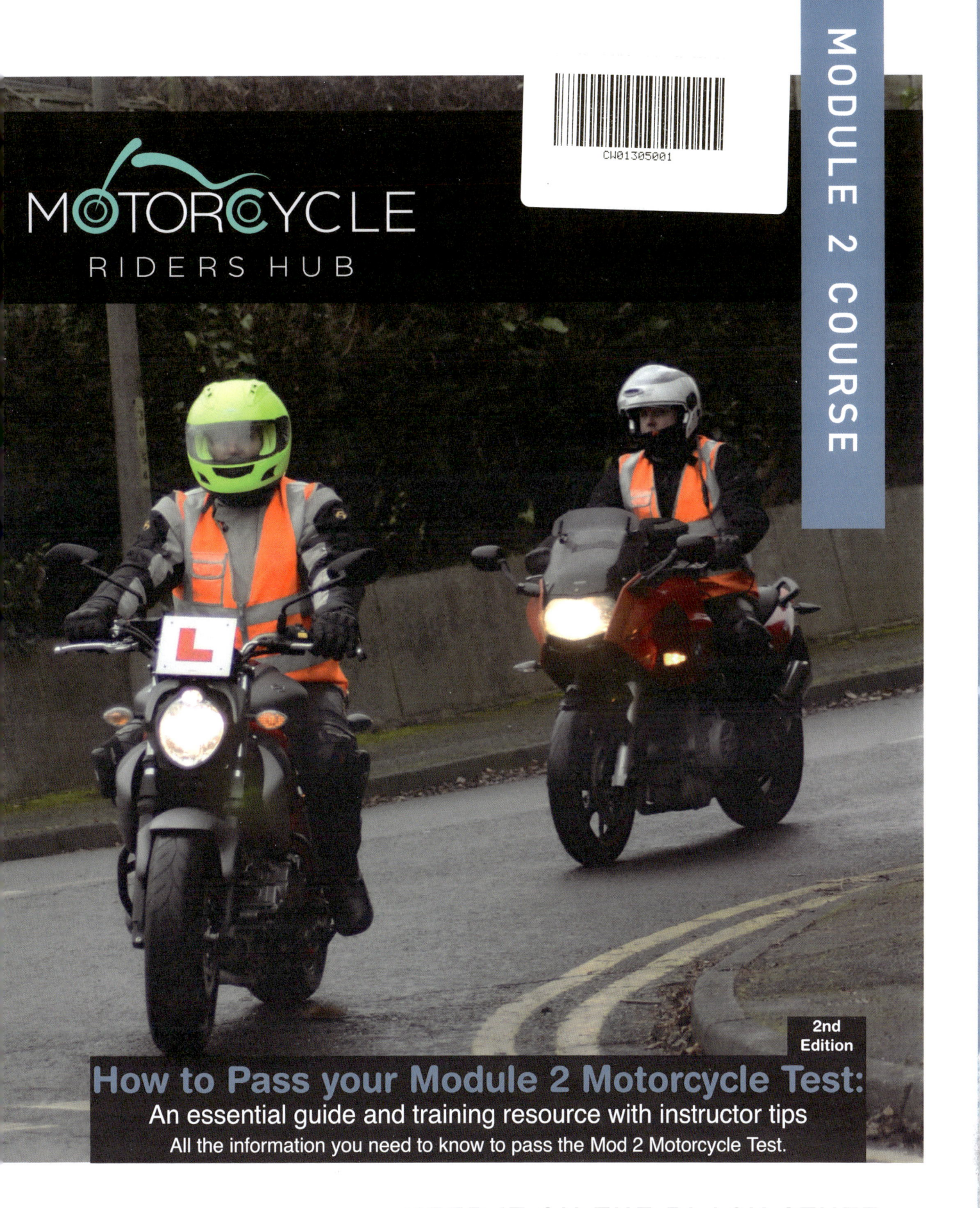

2nd Edition

How to Pass your Module 2 Motorcycle Test:
An essential guide and training resource with instructor tips
All the information you need to know to pass the Mod 2 Motorcycle Test.

KEEP IT ON THE BLACK STUFF

MotorcycleRidersHub.co.uk

© MOTORCYCLE RIDERS HUB

First published May 2021

The contents of the Motorcycle Riders Hub Module 2 Course e-book are copyright © Motorcycle Riders Hub and must not be reproduced or distributed in any form, without express permission in writing with consent from Motorcycle Riders Hub.

The information contained in this e-book is accurate at the time of publication.

This e-book is intended to be used alongside the corresponding Motorcycle Riders Hub Academy and professional motorcycle training.

Use this document as a guide and learning platform to help enhance skills and knowledge. Use of this e-book is subject to Motorcycle Riders Hub terms and conditions.

KEEP IT ON THE BLACK STUFF

ABOUT SIMON HAYES

A full-time instructor since 1991, Simon Hayes is a highly experienced motorcycle instructor and well known within the industry. Simon's first six years as an instructor were spent teaching military personnel, where he had a 100% success rate and earned a reputation for high level training.

Since 1996 Simon has operated a respected multisite motorcycle training business covering Birmingham and the Midlands. Over thirty years of dedication to the highest possible standards of motorcycle training has forged a reputation for excellence. Simon has seen many changes and challenges affecting the industry, his own training school has continued to thrive and develop.

Over these decades Simon has covered over a million miles and personally delivered novice to advanced training to many thousands of bikers. Simon is also sought after UK wide as an accomplished instructor trainer and has introduced countless new motorcycle instructors to the sector. In addition, Simon maintains a busy diary of European Tours covering advanced riding on the continent, off road training, track day training, local club and charity rides.

Some years ago, Simon began to improve his students' motorcycle training experience through complementary video based training.

Through pre-course learning students are able to visualise motorcycle skills training and find that their practical training is greatly enhanced.

Over a ten year period, these video training resources were refined, resulting in a first edition being formally published and more widely available.

KEEP IT ON THE BLACK STUFF

ABOUT SIMON HAYES CONTINUED...

From the early video training on a DVD, the delivery has been changed and nurtured into Motorcycle Riders Hub. The UK's first 100% video based motorcycle training resource. As the founder of Motorcycle Riders Hub, Simon's vision is to enhance rider training and safety across the UK, empowering both new and experienced riders to continually improve their skills.

Simon believes that the Motorcycle Riders Hub resources should not be used in isolation and must not be viewed as a substitute for professional motorcycle training. To get the best out of the training resource, riders should use the video training and practical training in tandem to elevate their learning experience. Practical training alone does not give learner riders all the tools they need.

Motorcycle Riders Hub is supported by a number of full time trainers and other professional motorcyclists, as well as an Advisory Panel, they are all committed to road safety and the values of 'Keep it on the black stuff'.

As Motorcycle Riders Hub continues to develop, its aim is to give riders a useful dedicated e-learning platform. Simon's ambition is to reach as many new riders as possible countrywide to help and guide them to become better riders, his commitment to motorcycle training continues with an ongoing full schedule of practical courses.

Motorcycle Riders Hub
Keep it on the black stuff

KEEP IT ON THE BLACK STUFF

ABOUT MOTORCYCLE RIDERS HUB

Over the last couple of decades there have been significant changes to motorcycle training. The latest development in rider training saw the introduction and implementation of CBT, Module One and Module 2 motorcycle tests. The result has been a substantial uplift in learner riders skills and ability.

Our vision is to help learner riders at all levels to improve their knowledge, ability and skills by using an online e-learning platform to raise personal riding standards.

Motorcycle Riders Hub is the UK's only 100% online motorcycle video training resource helping learner riders through their Compulsory Basic Training (CBT), Direct Access, Module One and Module 2 motorcycle tests.

The online program of dedicated guidance and learning resources will help all riders to develop and enhance their skills, ensuring they are better and safer riders and can keep it on the black stuff.

KEEP IT ON THE BLACK STUFF

CONTENTS

Getting ready

1. Learning to ride — 6
2. Module 2 overview — 7
3. Course explained — 8
4. Health declaration — 10
5. Residency decleration — 11
6. Eco-safe riding — 12
7. Documents and clothing — 13
8. Rider faults and fails — 15
9. Arriving at the test centre — 17
10. Examiners briefing — 18
11. Eyesight test — 19
12. Pre-ride checks — 20
13. Motorcycle safety questions — 22
14. Pillion safety questions — 23

Key skills

15. Moving away — 25
16. Motorcycle control — 26
17. Rear observations — 28
18. Signals — 30
19. Obstructions — 31
20. Use of speed — 32
21. Following distances — 33
22. Maintaining progress — 34
23. Judgement — 35
24. Road positioning — 36
25. Pedestrian crossings — 37
26. Normal stop position — 38
27. Awareness and planning — 39
28. Bends and cornering — 40
29. Joining dual carriageways — 41
30. Leaving dual carriageways — 42
31. Overtaking single vehicles — 43

Key skills continued...

32. Overtaking large vehicles — 44
33. Overtaking multiple vehicles — 45
34. Turning left into one-way streets — 47
35. Turning right into one-way streets — 48
36. Turning left into side roads — 49
37. Turning right into side roads — 50
38. Turning left at T junctions — 52
39. Turning right at T junctions — 53
40. Turning left at roundabouts — 55
41. Straight on at roundabouts — 56
42. Turning right at roundabouts — 58
43. Use of motorcycle stands — 60
44. Response to signs — 61
45. Traffic lights — 62

Independent riding

46. Independent ride — 63
47. Returning to the test centre — 64
48. First time on the road — 65
49. Take responsibility — 66
50. Take further training — 67

KEEP IT ON THE BLACK STUFF

LEARNING TO RIDE

Biking is a fabulous pastime, people are learning to ride a motorcycle for economic reasons. On the whole, motorcycles are less expensive to purchase, tax and insure than cars. Taking account of the cost of learning, they offer a cheaper route to getting mobile.

Parking is generally easier and less expensive with a motorcycle. Bikes can also mean quicker travel, by allowing riders to minimise the frustrations of traffic congestion. Given these benefits, there is also a good case for motorcycles to be used as a greener mode of transport.

Riders must recognise and take responsibility for their own vulnerability on the roads. This requires an investment in good protective clothing, plus a commitment to both compulsory and further motorcycle training. On today's faster and congested roads, rider responsibility demands the highest levels of observation, anticipation and planning.

Compulsory Basic Training (CBT) is the starting point. It sets the minimum standard for new riders, allowing riders to ride unaccompanied on the road, it is effectively the lowest level of rider skill and rider safety. This contentious observation is supported by statistics that attribute most motorcycle accidents to rider error.

For new riders Compulsory Basic Training does not tick all the boxes of learning to ride a motorcycle. This is why the Module 1 and 2 were introduced, it is to give riders a better examination of their riding by an independent body.

However, passing the motorcycle test is the first rung of the ladder. Novice riders must realise that this is a starting point and not the end of their journey. This is when riders are most vulnerable, because they are now independent and mistakes could be costly.

KEEP IT ON THE BLACK STUFF

MODULE 2 OVERVIEW

The Module 2 (Mod 2) is the on road aspect of the Two part practical motorcycle test and is taken at designated DVSA test centres throughout the UK. Following on from Module One, the Module 2 motorcycle test is structured to assess that riders have sufficient skills to ride confidently and safely on the public highway and in varying traffic conditions.

Module 2 also assesses a rider's practical understanding of the Highway Code and how to deal with a variety of road hazards.

Module 2 Test routes may vary, although the test criteria follows the same format throughout the UK. With professional Module 2 motorcycle training, riders will be fully prepared.

Starting from the test centre the Module 2 Test takes around 40 minutes, during which time the examiner will assess the candidates riding ability in as many different scenarios as possible. It includes a ten minute independent ride, where candidates are asked to follow traffic signs or a series of directions.

The Module 2 Test can be booked directly via the DVSA, but it is advisable to book through a local motorcycle training school. Quality motorcycle instruction results in better prepared, more confident, safer and skilled learner riders, with higher first time pass rates.

Instructor Tip
Using Motorcycle Riders Hub as a training aid along with professional coaching is going to enhance your development as a new rider.

KEEP IT ON THE BLACK STUFF

COURSE EXPLAINED

The Module 2 Course is designed to compliment professional motorcycle training. It helps to develop a learner rider's skills and knowledge when undertaking a Module 2 training course with a qualified motorcycle instructor. Motorcycle Riders Hub does not recommend a DIY approach to Module 2 motorcycle training.

For students embarking on Module 2 training for the first time, there is a lot to learn. For those with limited riding experience, sufficient motorcycle training, complimented by the Motorcycle Riders Hub Module 2 Course will result in test success

Instructor Tip
Investing time in researching this course will give candidates an elevated learning experience.

The Module 2 Course has been produced by a team of experienced, skilled and qualified motorcycle instructors. It has been further enhanced through student feedback.

- ▶ Instructional video modules
- ▶ Example Module 2 mock test routes
- ▶ Podcast & audio lessons
- ▶ e-book
- ▶ Module 2 quizzes to measure progress
- ▶ Motorcycle Instructor safety related tips

KEEP IT ON THE BLACK STUFF

COURSE EXPLAINED CONTINUED...

The goal of the Module 2 Course is to develop a better skilled, more confident and safer rider. With video guidance, the course enhances a student's training experience with pre learning and the opportunity to experience and visualise the core skills required for Module 2 test.

> **Instructor Tips**
>
> Keep studying time down to 40 minute sections before taking a 10 minute break.
>
> Learn slowly and methodically, because inch by inch is a cinch, yard by yard is hard!

Students can watch the videos as many times as they like, plus listen to audio lessons and podcasts, read the e-book and complete progress quizzes. The result is an enhanced, better prepared, less stressed Module 2 experience, instructors are then able to train students to a higher level.

KEEP IT ON THE BLACK STUFF

HEALTH DECLARATION

Module 2 test candidates are required to sign a health declaration that effectively self-certifies that their health is good enough to take the Module 2 motorcycle test.

Driving licence holders have a legal obligation to inform the DVLA of certain illnesses and medical conditions that could affect their ability to drive or ride safely. The Module 2 health declaration ensures that the examiner has clarified the motorcycle rider's legal responsibility before the test commences.

Along with the legal responsibilities, common sense dictates that good health is something that riders should take seriously. Eyesight, hearing, balance, judgement, co-ordination and muscle control, all contribute to safe motorcycle riding. It's easy to understand how certain illnesses could adversely affect road safety and could result in a driving licence being revoked and the rider being banned.

Other health considerations include the person's consumption of alcohol and drugs (including prescription medications) and their potential negative impact on a rider's ability to ride safely.

Key health considerations include:

- Do not drink and ride
- Do not take drugs and ride
- Certain illnesses must be reported to the DVLA
- You must be in good health to ride a motorcycle

RESIDENCY DECLARATION

Only UK residents are entitled to complete a UK motorcycle test. Module 2 test candidates are required to read and sign the residency declaration before starting their test. Signing this residency declaration has legal implications and should not be signed fraudulently.

This declaration refers to the location of normal residency regarding personal and occupational ties.

For those who have moved to the UK from another European Country or European Economic Area, a riding test should not be sought unless there have been 185 days of UK residency during the last 12 months.

If the examiner is in any doubt regarding a candidate's residency, they will cancel the test, pending proof or evidence of residency.

Key points to remember:

- Ensure you read, understand and sign the declaration
- Do not fraudulently sign a residency declaration
- If there is any doubt, the test may be cancelled

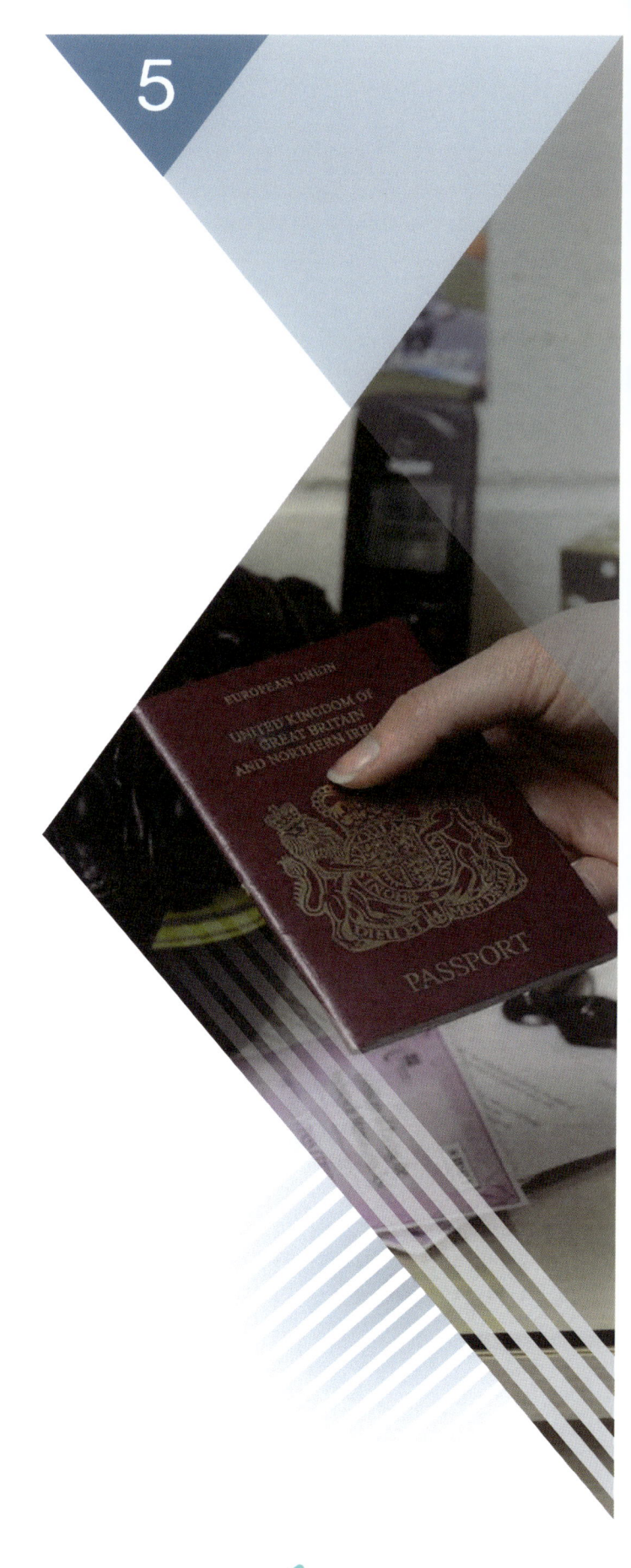

KEEP IT ON THE BLACK STUFF

ECO SAFE RIDING

We all have personal environmental responsibilities extending to the ecological impact of our riding, associated with consumption of fossil fuels and resulting in carbon footprint.

Riding in an eco-friendly way does not form part of the Module 2 test marking system, but the examiner is required to assess that a candidate is riding in an eco-friendly manner and at the end of the test may offer some advice on ways to improve eco-friendly riding skills.

An eco friendly way of riding involves effective forward planning and observation, so that inappropriate use of gears and aggressive braking are avoided. Over revving the engine, particularly when stationary and pulling away, should also be avoided.

If stopped for any length of time e.g. at a level crossing or roadworks, to improve fuel consumption and to avoid unnecessary pollution, riders should consider turning their engines off.

Key points to remember:

▶ Think and use effective forward planning

▶ Avoid aggressive acceleration and over revving

▶ Ensure appropriate use of gears and do not rush

▶ Ride smoothly and do not brake heavily

Instructor Tip
Always ride smoothly and safely to be in full control. This also reduces wear and tear on the motorcycle.

KEEP IT ON THE BLACK STUFF

DOCUMENTS AND CLOTHING

Module 2 Test preparations are essential. The key to successfully passing the Module Two test is the decision to undergo professional Module 2 Test training with a qualified motorcycle instructor.

Candidates must also ensure they wear the appropriate motorcycle clothing and have all their motorcycle documentation when going for test. The importance of getting things right is another good reason not to adopt a DIY approach to Module 2. Instead undergo professional guidance from a motorcycle training school.

Failure to wear the correct protective clothing or turn up with the right documentation will result in the Module 2 Test being cancelled and the test fee being lost.

Mandatory requirements:

- **Compulsory Basic Training (CBT) certificate** - in date and correctly filled out.

- **UK driving licence** - valid full or provisional UK photocard driving licence. Photographs are valid for ten years. Address must be correct (current living address). For paper licence holders (no photo-card), a valid UK passport is required.

- **Theory test certificate** - in date/valid motorcycle theory test pass certificate (valid for two years)

- **Module One pass certificate** - in date/valid Module One pass certificate (same expiry date as the theory test certificate).

- **Motorcycle** - must be same specification as used for Module One test. Must also be road legal, taxed, insured, have MOT if applicable and with full sized L plates to the front and rear.

- **Be on time** - there are no allowance for being late. Missing the allocated test slot will result in a cancelled Module 2 test and a lost test fee.

KEEP IT ON THE BLACK STUFF

DOCUMENTS AND CLOTHING CONTINUED...

Fully protective motorcycle clothing is highly recommended. Ideally, this should include leather motorcycle boots that provide a good level of ankle protection, along with armoured textile or leather motorcycle trousers and jacket. These should be worn with a motorcycle helmet (that meets current safety standards), plus quality motorcycle gloves and a high visibility vest.

Minimum acceptable clothing for test:
(if not using motorcycle clothing)

- **Motorcycle helmet** - that meets current safety standards

- **Sturdy footwear** - must support and protect ankles

- **Denim trousers** - heavy denim (no holes/tears)

- **Denim jacket** - heavy denim (no holes/tears), with several layers worn underneath

- **Motorcycle gloves** - good quality and condition

KEEP IT ON THE BLACK STUFF

RIDER FAULTS AND FAILS

The examiner will allow up to ten minor faults. Any major fault recorded will result in a Module 2 test failure. Minor faults are small rider errors that do not significantly impact on the road safety of the candidate, other road users or pedestrians.

Example minor faults include: positional errors, late indicating and in certain circumstances, missing an observation. All faults (major and minor) are recorded at the discretion of the examiner, whose decision must always be accepted.

Instructor Tip

If mistakes are made, leave them behind. Thinking about mistakes can lead to riding problems, ignore them and carry on.

In summary, any major fault will result in a fail. Less than ten minor faults (and no major faults) will, in most cases result in a pass. Recorded major faults (also classed as serious faults) will be discussed and explained at the end of the test.

If a fault is considered dangerous the examiner can terminate the test immediately. If this happens, the candidate will be required to dismount and wait with their motorcycle until their instructor collects them.

Major faults include:

- Failing the eyesight test
- Not having the correct documentation
- Failing to cancel a false indication
- Failing to carry out necessary lifesavers
- Actions that cause another vehicle to brake
- Actions that cause another vehicle to swerve
- Using the wrong lane
- Failing to stop for pedestrians on a zebra crossing
- Failing to stop at a red traffic light

KEEP IT ON THE BLACK STUFF

RIDER FAULTS AND FAILS CONTINUED...

Candidates are advised not to keep their own private score and to just continue with the Module 2 test, unless the examiner indicates otherwise.

Being negative by self analysis can result in unnecessary stress and even lead to a failure, even if all was going well.

> **Instructor Tip**
> It's how you deal with mistakes that really matters.

During the test candidates should relax, enjoy the ride and continue to the end without giving up. Regardless of the outcome, the experience is always valuable. When the Module 2 test has ended, the examiner will invite the candidate back into the test centre to debrief and complete the paperwork.

KEEP IT ON THE BLACK STUFF

ARRIVING AT THE TEST CENTRE

Arriving at the test centre fully prepared will result in a less stressed Module 2 test, with a higher chance of success. Being accompanied by a motorcycle instructor will help candidates manage their test centre arrival in the best way.

An experienced motorcycle instructor will know how best to park and position the motorcycle. They will ensure that the bike is positioned to commence the test, with good all round access to answer the motorcycle safety questions. A correctly positioned bike will allow access for the questions and enable the candidate to sit on exit the test centre easily.

Candidates are advised to turn up with plenty of time to spare. This ensures that the examiner is not kept waiting and that the test is not cancelled because of being late.

Arriving early also allows time to ask the instructor any last minute questions and carry out documentation checks. Candidates can also ensure their glasses and visor are clean, use the toilet, mentally prepare and calm their nerves.

Being accompanied by a qualified and experienced motorcycle instructor is the best practice. They can give guidance on the important elements of the Module 2 test which will result in less stress and a higher chance of a first time Module 2 test pass.

KEEP IT ON THE BLACK STUFF

EXAMINERS BRIEFING

With sufficient practice and an adequate number of Module 2 lessons, candidates should already know what to expect. Overall, 57 minutes are allocated to complete the Module 2 test. Depending on the test route, around 30-40 minutes are spent riding.

> **Instructor Tip**
> Listen carefully to the examiners instructions and ask questions to put your mind at rest.

Test routes are designed to cover a broad range of road and traffic scenarios, with varying speed limits, a variety of exercises and an independent ride.

The examiner's Module 2 test briefing is basic, clear and to the point.

General instructions include:

▶ Follow the road ahead at all times, unless the examiner or road signs direct otherwise

▶ Ride as independently as possible and try to forget about the examiner riding behind, who will give road directions but not instruction

▶ Where directions are not correctly implemented, the examiner will give corrective directions as required to return the candidate to the correct route

KEEP IT ON THE BLACK STUFF

EYESIGHT TEST

For obvious reasons failing the eyesight test is recorded as a major fault, and will result in a Module 2 test fail.

Glasses or contact lenses are allowed and candidates who have any doubt about their eyesight are advised to arrange an optician's eye check before booking a Module 2 test.

Candidates are required to read a number plate:

- In good daylight
- Containing letters/figures that are 79.4 mm (3.1 inches) high
- At a distance of 20.5 metres for vehicles with an old style number plate
- Or 20 metres for vehicles with a new style number plate
- With the aid of glasses or contact lenses (if normally worn)

> **Instructor Tip**
>
> Don't leave it till test day if you are unsure about your eyesight. Ask the training school to give you a practice check during training.

Candidates who are initially unable to read a number plate will be asked to sit in the waiting room whilst the examiner measures the exact distance with a tape measure. A second attempt at the exact measured distance will then be given. Candidates who fail the eyesight test on this second attempt will fail the Module 2 test and lose their test fee.

KEEP IT ON THE BLACK STUFF

PRE-RIDE CHECKS

Listen to and follow the examiners briefing and safety questions, the candidate will be invited to sit on their motorcycle and prepare to leave the test centre.

The examiner will then get ready on their own motorcycle. In most cases they will be following the candidate on a motorcycle but from time to time they have been known to conduct tests from a car. This is not the normal procedure, but does happen occasionally.

> **Instructor Tip**
>
> Take your time and don't rush. The examiner is not looking for a fast test time.

During the pre-ride checks candidates must not forget that the test has already started and the examiner is watching. As taught by the motorcycle instructor, candidates should carefully implement all required pre-ride checks before setting off.

Small things can make a big difference. The candidate should have the bike key to hand and should locate this in the ignition before putting on their gloves. Sometimes candidates rush and find themselves sat on the bike, gloves already on, but with the keys still in their pocket. Such things result in delays and unnecessary stress with the potential for other problems and minor faults.

Once on the bike, the side stand should be immediately stowed away, as the motorcycle could cut out when first gear is selected.

With the key in the ignition and the side stand up, the rider should adopt the safety position prior to starting the motorcycle.

A visual check that the engine cut out switch is in the correct position is also advised.

KEEP IT ON THE BLACK STUFF

PRE-RIDE CHECKS CONTINUED...

Before riding off candidates are advised to re-check mirror position (in case they have moved).

With the engine started the examiner will give a radio check and allow the volume to be adjusted if required. During the remainder of the test, further volume adjustments may be necessary.

With pre-ride checks complete, the examiner will direct the candidate to ride out of the test centre to start the Module 2 Test.

Instructor Tip

If your visor is steaming up, open it to clear the misting. If your view is impeded, safe decisiond cannot be made.

KEEP IT ON THE BLACK STUFF

MOTORCYCLE SAFETY QUESTIONS

Motorcycle safety checks are extremely important to road safety. Riders need to get to know their motorcycles well so that faults can be spotted early and before developing into more serious problems, especially ones that can have an impact on rider safety.

> **Instructor Tips**
>
> The chain should be checked at its tightest point (ask your trainer for more information)
>
> Ensure the chain oil/chain lube does not go onto the rear tyre.

Before starting the road ride, the examiner will ask a series of show me, tell me motorcycle safety questions.

These specific questions are available on the DVSA website and are covered in detail during Module 2 motorcycle training with professional training schools. This ensures that learner riders are prepared for their test and know how to fully check their own motorcycle.

Key points to remember:

▶ Learn the show me, tell me questions

▶ Learn how to look after a motorcycle

▶ Understand what each check is for

▶ Motorcycle training will cover these questions in detail

KEEP IT ON THE BLACK STUFF

PILLION SAFETY QUESTIONS

Along with the show me, tell me motorcycle safety questions, there is a Module 2 test requirement to understand how a motorcycle's balance can be affected by carrying a pillion passenger.

The examiner will ask one or two questions regarding the safety considerations of carrying a pillion passenger or load. These additional safety questions are usually asked at the beginning of the Module 2 Test.

> **Instructor Tip**
> Ensure any passenger receives a good brief before riding on the back, especially if they have never been a pillion before.

Failing to demonstrate an understanding of the balance and safety when carrying a pillion passenger may result in rider faults being added to the marking sheet, although this will not be advised until the very end of the test.

Sufficient Module 2 Test training with a qualified instructor should ensure that the safety questions are fully covered and prepared for.

Example pillion passenger safety questions:

- How would the motorcycle balance be affected by carrying a pillion passenger?
- How should you carry a pillion passenger?
- What problems could arise when carrying a pillion passenger?
- What advice should be given to an inexperienced pillion passenger?
- Legally, what is required to carry a pillion passenger?
- Before carrying a pillion passenger, what adjustments might be needed?

KEEP IT ON THE BLACK STUFF

PILLION SAFETY QUESTIONS CONTINUED...

Key points to remember:

- ▶ Cover these questions early to get familiar with the answers

- ▶ Practice the questions frequently and not just the night before the test

- ▶ A quick response to questions can get the test off to a good start

- ▶ Sufficient Module 2 Test training should ensure full preparation

- ▶ Candidates should ask the examiner to repeat the question if they need more thinking time

> **Instructor Tip**
> Always invite your passenger to get on and off, so that you are ready and can maintain balance and stability.

KEEP IT ON THE BLACK STUFF

MOVING AWAY

After pulling over or stopping, candidates are asked to move away when ready. The key part of this instruction is when ready and supports the importance of not rushing.

Candidates should select first gear, carry out effective all round observations, prepare to pull away and indicate if necessary. A lifesaver must then precede moving away.

> **Instructor Tip**
> Use plenty of throttle to avoid stalling the bike and slip the clutch, don't be in a hurry to move away.

Where possible, candidates should remain close to the kerb, because stalling would pose less of a road hazard than moving off at an angle and into the path of other road users.

Having pulled away successfully, cancel the signal and get up to speed so that any following traffic is not held up.

Key points to remember:

- Use good forward and rearward observations
- Signal if necessary and ensure it is clear
- Carry out a lifesaver before moving away
- Stay straight initially when pulling away, in case the bike stalls
- Cancel signal and get up to speed

KEEP IT ON THE BLACK STUFF

MOTORCYCLE CONTROL

Candidates must demonstrate good control throughout the Module 2 Test. This includes effective use of the five basic controls which are the clutch, throttle, gear lever, front and rear brake.

Good steering control, slow control manoeuvring along with correct use of switch gears, lights, indicators and the horn must also be used properly by the candidate.

Throttle control must be smooth, progressive and used with good clutch control to aid smooth gear changes and when using slow control.

Both brakes must be used safely and effectively throughout the test. Both brakes are used together, when the bike is upright, travelling in a straight line and slowing down from higher to lower speeds. The front brake should only be used when the bike is upright and travelling in a straight line. The rear brake is used on its own at slow speed or where there is input into the handlebars when steering or cornering.

> **Instructor Tip**
> Don't rush changing up the gears and fully release the clutch between each gear change.

In conjunction with braking and speed control, candidates must ensure the correct gears are Selected for good engine control, so that the bike does not labour or over rev.

At junctions, candidates must be in full control of the motorbike's position and demonstrate good steering control.

In bends, the examiner will be assessing the candidate's ability to corner safely by utilising effective steering, speed and position. Counter steering will ensure the bike is always in the correct position.

KEEP IT ON THE BLACK STUFF

MOTORCYCLE CONTROL CONTINUED...

Key points to remember:

- Use a flat wrist on the throttle to maintain full control
- Clutch control should be delicate and deliberate
- Always select the correct gear
- Use correct braking procedure throughout the test
- Good speed control is the key to effective steering
- Ensure good balance during slow control
- Use the ancillary controls where necessary
- Do not use the throttle aggressively
- Candidates should give themselves plenty of distance to slowdown

> **Instructor Tip**
> Balancing the clutch and throttle is imperative when steering out of the junctions using slow speed control.

KEEP IT ON THE BLACK STUFF

REAR OBSERVATIONS

Effective mirror checks, rear observations and lifesavers must be used throughout the Module 2 Test. Missed rear observations can be deemed as minor or major faults, but if lifesavers before moving position are habitually missed this will be recorded as a serious fault. This is categorised as a test fail!

> **Instructor Tip**
> Effective observations when moving position are necessary. Correctly timed lifesavers can save your life.

Professional pre-test Module 2 training is essential to fully learn the correct use of rear observations and to be spatially aware and safe on the road on a motorcycle.

All manoeuvres start with effective observations, allowing riders to gather information. Mirror checks will check what is happening directly behind and are required before signalling, altering speed, changing direction (a lifesaver is required as well), plus on approach to junctions and hazards.

When moving or stationary, a look over the right or left shoulder can be used to gather extra information e.g. when pulling away in a traffic queue or at a set of traffic lights.

> **Instructor Tip**
> Turning the head fully to look behind is not necessary, the mirrors inform the rider what is going on behind.

The examiner will expect to see effective lifesavers before moving position, moving around parked vehicles, pulling away from the side of the road and when navigating certain junctions.

KEEP IT ON THE BLACK STUFF

REAR OBSERVATIONS CONTINUED...

These final over the shoulder observations into the blind spot area can be to both the left and the right hand side.

With these rear observations, the rider must take care not to adversely affect their motorcycle's balance or position by altering the steering when turning their head.

Key points to remember:

- ▶ Check mirrors before signalling, changing speed and assessing behind
- ▶ Look over the shoulder to check blind spots
- ▶ Use a rearward observation to gather information
- ▶ Use a lifesaver before moving position, changing lanes, or turning

> **Instructor Tip**
> A lifesaver or rear observation is chin to shoulder, to check the blind spot.

KEEP IT ON THE BLACK STUFF

SIGNALS

The examiner will want to see effective signals that are appropriate, given in good time, not conflicting and cancelled on completion of the manoeuvre. Mistakes made while signals will result in faults being recorded. Failing to cancel a signal can be recorded as a major fault if it is deemed as conflicting or dangerous.

Signals inform other road users of an intended manoeuvre. They should be used when they are appropriate and required. Examples include: turning left or right at junctions when changing lanes and when moving off from the side of the road.

When there is no other traffic present, signals are not always required. Candidates must always be careful not to give false indications or signals that are conflicting to other road users.

Correctly timed signals are important to other road users understanding the rider's intention. Being precise with a signal will ensure there is enough time for others to react.

Candidates should avoid indicating too early for a junction, where there is a side road on the same side of the road, prior to the end of the road.

Key points to remember:

- ▶ Failing to cancel a signal can be a major fault
- ▶ Signals inform other road users of an intended manoeuvre
- ▶ Avoid giving false or conflicting signals
- ▶ Signals must be given in a timely manner
- ▶ Poor planning can result in incorrect signalling
- ▶ Never leave signals to the last second
- ▶ Use signals when leaving a roundabout
- ▶ Cancel a false indication and reapply if necessary

KEEP IT ON THE BLACK STUFF

OBSTRUCTIONS

Obstructions include parked cars, road works, oncoming vehicles, open car doors, pedestrians, horses and anything else that hinders normal road position.

Clearance is the safe space and distance the rider creates to reduce risk, while maintaining safe and controlled progress.

Where there are obstructions, the examiner needs to see good forward and rearward observations, along with good judgement, positioning, appropriate use of speed and adequate clearance around the obstruction. Such actions may require a move into the opposing lane, with good forward planning to ensure there is no oncoming traffic and a safe route back to the correct position. These manoeuvres require a lifesaver before moving position.

Most test routes are chosen to include roads where obstructions are common and moving to clear obstructions correctly is essential.

A local Module 2 training provider will prepare candidates to deal safely with challenging local road situations while practicing for the test.

Key points to remember:

- Look and plan well ahead
- Use good all-round observation
- Ensure adequate clearance from obstructions
- Use effective mirror checks and lifesavers
- Look for people walking between vehicles
- Horses need extra room and low engine noise
- Good forward vision is essential

KEEP IT ON THE BLACK STUFF

USE OF SPEED

In conjunction with understanding road signs and road markings, the examiner will assess compliance with speed limits. A variety of speed limits will be encountered from 20mph, that may be in force near schools, up to national speed limits of 70mph on dual carriageways.

> **Instructor Tip**
> The examiner isn't looking for a fast ride, just an appropriate and safe speed for the prevailing conditions.

Although the examiner will expect candidates to make appropriate progress, speed limits must not be seen as a target. The assessment of a student's use of speed primarily relates to road safety.

Road surface, weather conditions and traffic flow all have a bearing on speed, as does riding experience and ability. Candidates must travel at speeds that are appropriate to the road and traffic conditions and their own ability but not breaking any speed limits.

Failure to observe speed limits and/or riding at speeds that exceed rider ability will likely result in a test fail.

Key points to remember:

- Always observe speed limits
- Do not see speed limits as a target
- Do not ride at speeds that exceed ability
- Too much speed equals less time to react
- Always use smooth throttle control

KEEP IT ON THE BLACK STUFF

FOLLOWING DISTANCES

The examiner will assess the candidate's observation of a safe following distance. Correct distances allow the rider time to react safely to whatever happens ahead of them i.e. stopping without the need for an emergency stop.

Following distances change because of the rider's speed, weather, road surface, traffic flow and sometimes the size of the vehicle being followed.

A general rule is one metre per mile an hour of speed, so travelling at 30mph would indicate a following distance of at least 30 metres.

Another way is to use the two second rule where riders should not be closer than two seconds from the vehicle in front. Some motorcycle trainers suggest saying out loud, only a fool breaks the two second rule, which takes around two seconds to say. In wet conditions following distances must be doubled to four seconds.

When stopping behind stationary vehicles, at least a car length is required from a car, with more distance needed behind larger vehicles. Behind vans, buses and trucks, riders must stop at a distance that gives a clear view of the wing mirrors of the vehicle in front.

Key points to remember:

▶ Allow sufficient following distance to always be able to react safely

▶ Apply the two second rule in dry conditions - doubled in the wet

▶ Allow sufficient distance behind stationary vehicles

▶ Always be able to see the wing mirror of larger stationary vehicles in front

KEEP IT ON THE BLACK STUFF

MAINTAINING PROGRESS

Maintaining progress requires good vision, planning and use of speed. Too much speed, especially approaching junctions and in traffic, can result in problems, excessive braking or not being able to stop safely.

The examiner will assess the rider's use of speed, slow control, observation and planning in respect of how the candidate maintains progress throughout the Module 2 Test. Not maintaining progress can result in both minor and/or major faults being recorded.

Candidates will need to understand the difference between open and closed junctions, plus how to correctly approach and look early into junctions. Practice is crucial and candidates are encouraged to undertake professional Module 2 training prior to the motorcycle test.

Candidates are also advised to ride for themselves and as if not being followed by an examiner. It is the examiner's responsibility to keep up with the test candidate.

Key points to remember:

- ▶ Use good observation, planning and speed
- ▶ Look early into junctions and use slow control
- ▶ Maintain progress and avoid stopping unnecessarily
- ▶ Don't wait for big gaps for you and the examiner, the candidate should ride for themselves at all times

KEEP IT ON THE BLACK STUFF

JUDGEMENT

The examiner will be assessing how well a candidate judges movement, speed and available space in relation to other road users. Use of all round observation, forward planning and judgement are key skills in making the correct decisions to avoid danger.

The examiner will look for good judgement when passing or overtaking and that enough clearance is given. Consideration must be given to car doors that might open, oncoming vehicles and locating a safe return space back into position.

Filtering is an uncommon test requirement at most test locations, but requires the same judgement and decisions to pass parked vehicles.

Crucial to the riders judgement is good all round observations. The examiner will expect to see lifesavers, mirror checks and rear observations when required. Good judgement is also key to manoeuvres that involve crossing the path of other vehicles, such as turning right into a side road.

Key points to remember:

► Stop if unsure, always be safe

► Always allow plenty of clearance

► Do not squeeze through small gaps

► Always plan a safe return space

► Use good all round observation

► Don't take risks

► Candidates must ride for themselves

ROAD POSITIONING

The candidate's road positioning is also assessed by the examiner, who will want to see good positioning that ensures the safest route.

Positioning requires good observation, constant planning and positioning in respect to other vehicles, the road surface, weather conditions, visibility, junctions and the road ahead.

Novice riders taking a Module 2 Test only need to use three positions. These are: central (neutral position), left hand side of the lane and right hand side of the lane.

Choosing a central position makes the rider more visible to other road users and allows more room for adjustment. In the event of rider error, there is room for steering errors and drifting out of position.

Positioning to the right or left may be required to avoid a hazard on the road surface, to move away from a developing hazard involving other vehicles, to show intentions on the road when signalling, to maintain a dominant road position or to maximise rider visibility to road users ahead. Always position for safety.

Key points to remember:

- Ride centrally in the lane
- Move left to turn left - use the left wheel track
- Move right to turn right - use the right wheel track
- A wheel track is where car tyres would normally be

Instructor Tip
The safest position is always correct but the correct position is not always safest.

KEEP IT ON THE BLACK STUFF

PEDESTRIAN CROSSINGS

Candidates must understand the various types of pedestrian crossing. These include: zebra, toucan, pelican, puffin and pegasus crossings, along with safe havens and manned situations i.e. children's crossings under the control of a school crossing patrol, traffic warden or police officer.

An awareness of local test routes and a knowledge of the types of crossings that may be encountered is a good idea. This, along with professional instruction on how to approach various crossings, can be covered by booking Module 2 training with a local motorcycle training school.

The important thing to remember is pedestrian crossings are for pedestrians to cross roads safely.

Candidates should anticipate people's actions and adopt a slow enough speed to stop safely. Care should be taken where street furniture, parked or queuing vehicles are obscuring a crossing.

Consideration should be extended to elderly and infirm pedestrians who may take longer to cross. Failure to stop, if required to do so at pedestrian crossings will result in a test fail.

Key points to remember:

▶ Always stop at a zebra crossing if someone is waiting to cross

▶ If approaching traffic lights expect the lights to change, especially if someone is waiting

▶ Toucan, puffin, pelican and pegasus crossings are all controlled by traffic lights

▶ Be vigilant when approaching crossing, some people cross away from the designated area

KEEP IT ON THE BLACK STUFF

NORMAL STOP POSITION

The examiner will ask the candidate to pull over and stop several times during the Module 2 test. A key part of the instruction given will always be when it is safe to do so. Candidates should not feel pressured to stop straight away.

Ideally, pull over on a straight section of road, but not close to or opposite a junction or bus stop. Bends should also be avoided, as should the base or brow of a hill, along with driveways and yellow or red painted lines.

> **Instructor Tip**
> The examiner may request you pull over in a designated position.

A safe normal stop also requires planning, an indication, observation and moving to the left hand side of the lane towards the kerb. Candidates must remember that an instruction to stop will always be followed by an instruction to pull away safely, after the stop has been carried out. Both manoeuvres have the potential for minor and major faults.

Key points to remember:

- Stop on a straight road
- Do not stop opposite a hazard
- Stop where there is a raised kerb
- Only pull over and stop when safe to do so
- Think ahead and about pulling away, when looking for a safe place to stop

> **Instructor Tip**
> The examiner may request you pull over in a designated position.

KEEP IT ON THE BLACK STUFF

AWARENESS AND PLANNING

Awareness and planning skills improve with time and experience and further motorcycle training.

Novice riders tend not to look far enough ahead with good forward vision, but instead spend too much time looking at their motorcycle controls and at the road directly ahead of their motorcycle.

During the Module 2 Test, most situations a candidate finds themselves in are dependent on good vision, awareness and planning. The examiner will be assessing this to ensure the candidate is looking far enough ahead, whilst using effective rear observations and lifesavers.

Candidates must use correct observations to be aware of their surroundings, the road ahead, potential hazards and other road users.

Good awareness allows continuous planning, through judging and anticipating what other road users are doing and taking appropriate actions to remain safe. Candidates must look well ahead to be able to deal with hazards in good time.

Key points to remember:

▶ Always look and plan well ahead

▶ Good vision and all round observations are essential

▶ React early and in plenty of time

▶ Be aware of cyclists and horse riders

▶ Consider personal ability, weather and traffic condition

▶ Be aware of vulnerable road users, such as children and elderly people

KEEP IT ON THE BLACK STUFF

BENDS AND CORNERING

Novice riders must approach corners with care, use good forward observation of road signs and visual clues. Lamp posts, telegraph pylons and tree lines can be used to assess a corner's severity. Road surface, camber and other hazards must be taken into account. Candidates should slow down on approach and adopt an appropriate speed and gear.

On approach apply the brakes before cornering, avoid braking during the corner itself. Never use the front brake whilst the bike is leaning over or cornering. If there is a need to slow down whilst cornering, this should be done by closing the throttle and lightly applying the rear brake only.

The examiner wants to see candidates adjust their speed correctly before cornering and not braking in bends. Candidates should remain in the centre of the lane, but can if required move to avoid a hazard in the road, staying away from the oncoming traffic and manhole covers, or debris in the road.

Professional motorcycle training and practice are recommended to help master cornering and counter steering. Candidates must fully understand these skills before taking their Module 2 Test.

Key points to remember:

- Adjust speed before reaching a bend
- Adopt the correct gear before the corner
- Avoid braking in a corner, especially the front brake
- Look out for loose road surface whilst cornering

KEEP IT ON THE BLACK STUFF

JOINING DUAL CARRIAGEWAYS

Slip lanes leading onto the dual carriageways allow the candidate to match their speed and to merge safely with traffic already on the dual carriageway. Judgement, positioning and maintaining progress are used in conjunction with good forward observation, along with mirror checks and a lifesaver to move into a safe gap.

Although indicating early communicates the rider's intention, giving way to vehicles already on the dual carriageway is still imperative before a rider can join the nearside lane.

A final lifesaver before changing lanes is important and as with any other give-way junction, if it is not safe to proceed, a rider should plan to stop at the very end of the slip lane as a last resort for safety.

Once on the dual carriageway, riders should cancel the signal and accelerate to an appropriate speed.

Key points to remember:

- Good planning and observation are required
- Use LADA: Look, Assess, Decide, Act
- Signal early to join
- Match speed and find a safe gap to merge into
- Always give way and if required stop
- Final lifesaver before changing lanes
- Once joined, cancel signal and get up to a safe speed

Instructor Tip
The way to improve the required skills is to practice under tuition.

LEAVING DUAL CARRIAGEWAYS

Leaving a dual carriageway usually happens via a slip lane, which will normally be long enough to allow safe deceleration from higher speeds.

Riders must use good forward observation, judgement, positioning and an early indication to inform other road users (in good time) that they intend to leave the dual carriageway.

> **Instructor Tip**
> Slow down on the dual carriageway if there is a short slip lane, or there are adverse weather conditions.

Where possible, do not slow down on the dual carriageway, this is what the slip lane is for. Keep an eye in the mirrors to see what the traffic flow is like behind, move across into the slip lane as early as possible, cancel the signal and then slow down using the brakes on the slip lane to deal with the possible corner and junction at the end.

Key points to remember:

- Look and plan well ahead
- Signal early to warn following vehicles
- Avoid slowing down on the dual carriageway
- Cancel signal after moving into the slip lane
- Use both brakes to slow down

KEEP IT ON THE BLACK STUFF

OVERTAKING SINGLE VEHICLES

Riders should use the driving lane (left hand lane) and only use the overtaking lane (right hand lane) to overtake slower moving traffic.

Riders should not stay in the overtaking lane for longer than is necessary and once the overtake is complete, they should move back to the left hand lane.

> **Instructor Tip**
> Stay in the centre of the overtaking lane, when overtaking.

When moving out to overtake, ensure it is safe to do so with regular mirror checks to gather information behind. Indicate early and let it flash at least 5-6 times to make other vehicles aware of the intention to change lanes. When it is safe, carry out a lifesaver to move out, cancel signal, complete the overtake and when clear of the slower moving vehicle, take a mirror check and lifesaver over the left shoulder and move back in.

Key points to remember:

- Maintain at least two seconds from the vehicle in front
- Signal early and let it flash at least 5-6 times
- Effective mirror checks and a right hand lifesaver to move out
- Cancel signal and complete the overtake
- Once clear carry out a left lifesaver to move back in

> **Instructor Tip**
> Never rush to move position when overtaking.

KEEP IT ON THE BLACK STUFF

OVERTAKING LARGE VEHICLES

In general riders are advised to use the driving lane (left hand lane) most of the time and to only move into the overtaking lane (right hand lane) when overtaking slower moving vehicles.

When overtaking large vehicles, riders can experience quite severe buffeting from downdrafts, along with visual issues caused by road spray (if it is wet).

On approach, care should be taken with no less than a two second following distance (in dry conditions), be aware of the driver's limited view in their wing mirrors. Overtaking in a central position is best, as it allows more room for error and buffeting.

When moving out to overtake, ensure it is safe with regular mirror checks to gather information behind. Indicate early and let it flash at least 5-6 times to make other vehicles aware of the overtake.

When it is safe, carry out a right lifesaver to move out, cancel signal and complete the overtake. Once the overtake is complete and when clear of the slower moving larger vehicle, take a mirror check and left lifesaver to move back in.

Key points to remember:

▶ Signal early and let it flash at least 5-6 times

▶ Effective mirror checks and a right hand lifesaver to move out

▶ Once clear carry out a left lifesaver to move back in

▶ Stay central in the adopted lane

Instructor Tip
It may be necessary to move to the right hand side of the overtaking lane for larger vehicles.

KEEP IT ON THE BLACK STUFF

OVERTAKING MULTIPLE VEHICLES

Riders are advised to use the driving lane (left hand lane) most of the time and to only move into the overtaking lane (right hand lane) when overtaking slower moving vehicles. Whichever lane is used, a central position in that lane is advised.

> **Instructor Tip**
> While overtaking for longer periods of time, it is imperative to maintain good awareness behind with regular mirror checks.

Overtaking multiple vehicles requires looking as far ahead as possible, to be aware that a safe return space exists.

Consideration must be given to the types of vehicle being overtaken i.e. larger vehicles have the potential for downdrafts and spray (in the wet).

Judgement may also be required in respect of the relative speeds of vehicles, in case one is showing signs of moving out or accelerating.

Rear observations are used to check there are no faster moving vehicles coming up behind.

During the overtake, when in the right hand lane, a central position in the lane is best for novice riders.

> **Instructor Tip**
> Do not move quickly from lane to lane during and after the overtake.

When moving out to overtake, ensure it is safe, with regular mirror checks to gather information behind.

OVERTAKING
MULTIPLE VEHICLES CONTINUED...

Indicate early and let it flash at least 5-6 times to make other vehicles aware of the intention to move lanes. When it is safe carry out a right lifesaver to move out, cancel the signal and continue with the overtake.

Once the overtake is complete and when clear, take a left mirror check and lifesaver and move back into the central position of the driving lane.

> **Instructor Tip**
> Carry out overtakes in good time and not just before exiting the dual carriageway.

Key points to remember:

- ▶ Maintain at least two seconds from the vehicle(s) in front in dry conditions
- ▶ Signal early, and let it flash at least 5-6 times
- ▶ Effective mirror checks and a right hand lifesaver to move out
- ▶ Cancel signal in the overtaking lane and complete the overtake
- ▶ Once clear carry out a left lifesaver to move back in

KEEP IT ON THE BLACK STUFF

TURNING LEFT INTO ONE WAY STREETS

A good understanding of signs and road markings as shown in the Highway Code, helps candidates to identify both ends of one way streets.

A candidate's response to one way street markings and signs can be put to the test by the examiner giving directions that could trip up poorly prepared candidates.

When turning left in a one way street, either at a T-junction or into a side road, candidates are advised to use the OSMPSL routine and position left of the centre whilst negotiating the junction.

When turning left into a one way street (side road), use the left hand lane on entry but if necessary it is acceptable to move straight into the right hand lane. This could be because of parked vehicles in the left hand lane.

Turning left at a T-junction in a one way street is the same as a normal left turn at the end of a road.

Key points to remember:

▶ Use the OSMPSL routine

▶ Be sure to understand one way signs and road markings

▶ Position early and be aware of overtaking vehicles

▶ When turning into side roads, it's ok to use the right hand lane if necessary

Instructor Tip
Follow the line of the kerb, when turning left.

KEEP IT ON THE BLACK STUFF

TURNING RIGHT INTO ONE WAY STREETS

A good understanding of signs and road markings as shown in the Highway Code helps with identifying both ends of one-way streets. A candidate's response to one-way street markings and signs can be assessed by the examiner, giving directions that could trip up poorly prepared candidates.

When turning right in a one way street either at a T-junction or into a side road, candidates are advised to use the OSMPSL routine and position right of centre whilst negotiating the junction.

When turning right into a one way street (side road), use the left hand lane on entry where possible, but if necessary it is acceptable to move straight into the right hand lane i.e. if there are parked vehicles in the left hand lane.

Turning right at a T-junction in a one way street is a mirror image of the left turn. A candidate should move towards the right hand kerb on approach and angle the bike to the right at the mouth of the junction. Following the line of the kerb will help achieve the correct position when exiting the junction.

Key points to remember:

- ▶ Use the OSMPSL routine on approach
- ▶ Be sure to understand one way signs and road markings
- ▶ Position in the right hand lane, it is a mirror image of turning left
- ▶ It's ok to use the right hand lane if the left lane has parked vehicles when turning into side roads

TURNING LEFT INTO SIDE ROADS
(LEFT TURN: MAJOR TO MINOR)

Left turns tend to be easier for novice riders. Candidates must use the OSMPSL routine, reduce speed in plenty of time, adopt the correct road position and look early into the junction to assess all hazards. The examiner is likely to say, "take the next road on the left please."

Riders will normally position slightly left of centre in the left wheel track, but need to be aware of road surface hazards i.e. drain covers, leaves, loose gravel and parked vehicles. Maintain good rearward observations and be aware of overtaking traffic, as other vehicles may try to pass.

An alternative position is to stay in the centre of the lane and to dominate the road on approach to the junction. Local motorcycle training providers will have their own views on correct junction position and their advice should be taken.

An instructor's local road knowledge on test routes is essential when dealing with obscure junctions, when preparing for the Module 2 Test.

Key points to remember:

► Also, known as left turn - major to minor

► Ensure correct position and protect road space

► Adopt the correct speed on approach

► Follow kerb line around at the junction for good position

► Do not accelerate too early to avoid drifting wide

Instructor Tip
Look out for pedestrians crossing in the side roads.

KEEP IT ON THE BLACK STUFF

TURNING RIGHT INTO SIDE ROADS
(RIGHT TURN: MAJOR TO MINOR)

Turning right into a side road can be a difficult turn for novice riders. The required position is to the right of the lane, in the right hand wheel track.

Candidates must also give way to oncoming traffic, along with rearward observations to check for road users who are trying to overtake or undertake.

The OSMPSL routine is required, along with slow control in the final approach and looking early into the junction. Candidates must signal at the appropriate time, adopt the correct speed and gear, put the bike in the correct position and ensure good all round observations on approach.

> **Instructor Tip**
> A lifesaver is imperative to rider safety before turning right across a carriageway, the right lifesaver must be correctly timed.

All hazards must be considered i.e. the road surface, drain covers, parked vehicles and pedestrians.

When near to the junction and it is clear, do a right lifesaver at around two car lengths from the turning point. This gives time to look forward, assess the road ahead, while there is still enough space to either turn safely or stop. If stopping, another lifesaver is required before continuing.

Once in the new lane the candidate should cancel the signal and proceed into the new road.

> **Instructor Tip**
> Use the clutch to control the speed and ensure smooth delivery of power.

TURNING RIGHT
INTO SIDE ROADS CONTINUED...

Key points to remember:

▶ Known as 'right turn - major to minor'

▶ Use the OSMPSL routine

▶ Ensure correct position on approach to protect road space

▶ Maintain the correct speed on approach

▶ Always be prepared to stop

▶ Lifesaver before committing to right turn

▶ Take time and do not rush

▶ Avoid cutting the corner or turning late and *swan necking

▶ When safe, make the turn, under control and safely

* Check with local motorcycle trainer for definition of swan necking and the right corner cut to understand the problems it can cause.

Instructor Tip
"Look out for pedestrians crossing in the side roads."

KEEP IT ON THE BLACK STUFF

TURNING LEFT AT T JUNCTIONS
(LEFT TURN: MINOR TO MAJOR)

Turning left at T-junctions is commonly encountered on the test. The examiner will most likely say, "at the end of the road, turn left please".

The OSMPSL routine must be used. Candidates should indicate early, slow down in plenty of time and look early into the junction, ensuring good road position and be ready to stop or ride on if clear.

Candidates normally need to position slightly left, in the left wheel track but taking note of road surface problems, parked vehicles and any other hazards.

Being vigilant and looking out for overtaking traffic by using good mirror checks. Once at the junction, if stationary, be aware of other road users trying to overtake.

Key points to remember:

- Known as a left turn - minor to major
- Use the OSMPSL routine on approach
- Ensure correct position and protect road space
- Make sure of correct speed on approach
- Always be ready to stop at the junction
- A car length away either look forward and stop or look in the direction of travel and ride on
- Follow the kerb line around at the junction to maintain a good position
- When safe to do so, continue out of the junction slowly and under control

Instructor Tip
Once in the new lane cancel signal before moving away.

TURNING RIGHT AT T JUNCTIONS

(RIGHT TURN: MINOR TO MAJOR)

Turning right at a T-junction requires the OSMPSL routine. Slowing down to a slow speed is essential to look early into the junction and in both directions.

Turning right at a T-junction can be challenging for novice riders. The examiner will most likely say, "at the end of the road, turn right please".

On approach give an appropriate signal, position early if possible and slow down using both brakes. At the point where slow control is required, use the rear brake only, approaching the junction the candidate must give way in both directions.

> **Instructor Tip**
> Once the decision is made, look in the direction of travel. Make sure the speed is controlled using the clutch.

Be ready to give way to traffic at the junction, unless there is a stop sign and it is then necessary to stop. Approach at a slow speed, in the correct gear and use the best position, which should allow a decision to be made by looking into the junction early. Continue out of the junction if safe to do so.

Regular rearward observations are required on approach to the junction, in case other road users try to under or overtake. If the decision is made to stop at the end of the road, a lifesaver may be required before moving on.

Pull out slowly and under control, avoid riding quickly as this will make the bike run wide. Once in the new lane, cancel the signal before accelerating away.

KEEP IT ON THE BLACK STUFF

TURNING RIGHT
AT T JUNCTIONS CONTINUED...

> **Instructor Tip**
> "Don't go too close to the white line in the centre of the road."

Key points to remember:

- Also known as right turn - minor to major
- Use the OSMPSL routine
- Position correctly on approach to protect road space
- Adopt the correct speed and position on approach
- Always be prepared to stop at the junction
- Decide a car length from the junction to look forward and stop in first gear, behind the white line, or look forward in the direction of travel and ride out
- Aim slightly to the right at the mouth of the junction
- When clear, ride out slowly, under control and safely with correct steering control

> **Instructor Tip**
> Never rush at a junction to beat the approaching traffic.

TURNING LEFT AT ROUNDABOUTS

Most roundabouts have four individual junctions, sometimes referred to as a four spoke roundabout.

The OSMPSL routine is required for approaching roundabouts. Candidates must use the correct speed, select the correct gear and allow sufficient time to position properly whilst looking into the roundabout to assess traffic.

The examiner will most likely say, "at the roundabout turn left, the first exit please."

Turning left at a roundabout is similar to turning left at a T-junction, but use a central position in the required lane to prevent vehicles squeezing past.

Reduce speed and gears on approach and when close enough transfer to the rear brake only before reaching the roundabout.

Look to the right on approach to assess if it is clear to continue. Stop if necessary behind the white line in the centre of the lane and in first gear.

When it is clear to move off, stay in the centre of the desired lane in the roundabout, locate and move into the new lane and then cancel signal.

Key points to remember:

- ▶ Ensure correct position to protect road space
- ▶ Reduce speed on approach
- ▶ Be prepared to stop at the junction if necessary
- ▶ Always stop if there is any question of safety
- ▶ Take time and do not be pressured
- ▶ Remain in the centre of left hand lane on approach

KEEP IT ON THE BLACK STUFF

STRAIGHT ON AT ROUNDABOUTS

The examiner will say, "at the roundabout follow the road ahead, the second exit please." Candidates must use the OSMPSL routine and approach at a comfortable speed, in the correct gear and adopt a dominant position in the centre of their lane.

Take note of road markings and if there are none, use the left hand lane. The approach is the same as for turning left, but without the need to indicate which communicates the intention to ride straight ahead.

Instructor Tips
Ask the local training provider to fully explain the term the point of no return.

Also clarify which shoulder a lifesaver should be taken depending on prevailing conditions.

Look early into the roundabout and once the decision to go is made move into the centre of the left hand lane (outer lane).

On reaching the point of no return, apply the left signal to show the intention to leave the roundabout. Carry out a lifesaver to check it is safe to leave and then exit into the new lane. Once in the new lane cancel signal and continue.

Instructor Tip
Avoid gravel build up in certain areas on the outside of the roundabout.

Professional motorcycle training is essential, especially for dealing with complicated roundabouts.

A local training provider will ensure candidates know how to deal safely with various roundabouts on possible test routes and take training before taking the Module 2 Test.

STRAIGHT ON AT ROUNDABOUTS CONTINUED...

> **Instructor Tip**
> An awareness check over the right shoulder maybe necessary before exiting the roundabout.

Key points to remember:

- Use OSMPSL routine on approach
- Ensure correct position to protect road space
- Adopt the correct speed on approach
- Always be prepared to stop at the roundabout
- Stay in the middle of the outer (left hand) lane for safety
- Take sufficient time and do not rush
- In the roundabout, avoid cutting across into the inner lane
- A lifesaver must be taken before leaving the roundabout

> **Instructor Tip**
> Do not drift into the right hand lane in the roundabout.

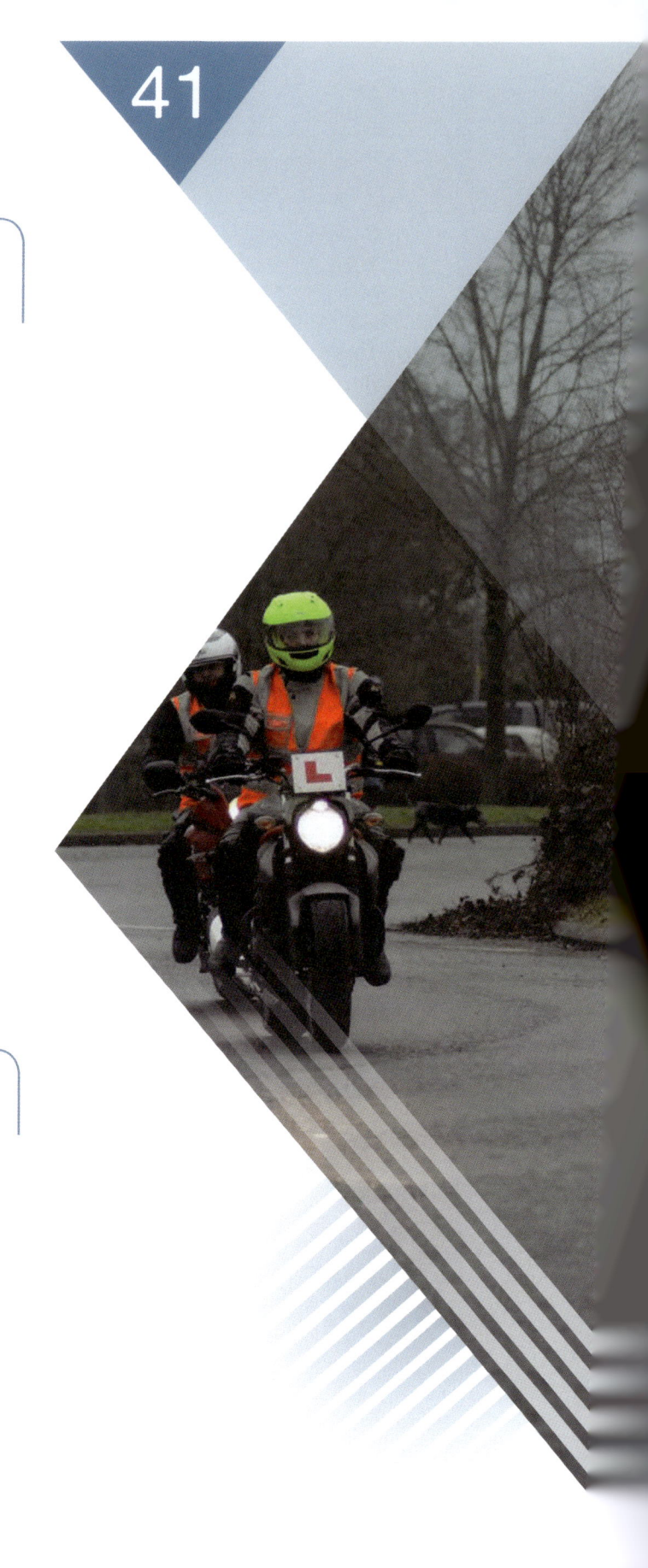

KEEP IT ON THE BLACK STUFF

TURNING RIGHT AT ROUNDABOUTS

The examiner will most likely say "at the roundabout turn right, the third exit please".

The OSMPSL routine must be used on approach. Take note of road markings and if none are present, use the right hand lane.

Indicate right and move into the middle of the right hand lane, maintaining a dominant lane position to prevent other vehicles from trying to squeeze through.

> **Instructor Tip**
> Should the wrong lane be chosen on approach to the roundabout, that direction should be taken for rider safety.

Approach the roundabout at an appropriate speed, in the correct gear and in a central position in the right hand lane. Look early into the roundabout, assess the traffic and decide to ride on if clear, or stop if not (or in any doubt).

The final approach should be on the rear brake only and stop if necessary behind the white line, in the centre of the lane, in first gear.

Once a decision to go is made, move into the centre of the right hand lane (inner lane). It may be necessary to take a lifesaver to the left on entering the roundabout. Do not cut across the left hand lane.

> **Instructor Tip**
> Do not change your mind where to go once in the roundabout.

Once in a central position in the right hand lane (inner lane), continue to look in the intended direction of travel and on reaching the point of no return, change signal to the left and carry out a left lifesaver in preparation to exit the roundabout. Once in the new lane, cancel the signal.

TURNING RIGHT AT ROUNDABOUTS CONTINUED...

This type of roundabout can be challenging for novice riders and it is advisable to undertake professional motorcycle training prior to taking the Module 2 Test.

Key points to remember:

- ▶ Use the OSMPSL routine on approach
- ▶ Adopt the correct position to protect road space
- ▶ Maintain correct speed on approach
- ▶ Be prepared to stop at the roundabout
- ▶ Stay in the middle of the inner (right) lane
- ▶ Take time and do not rush
- ▶ Do not cut across left lane in the roundabout
- ▶ Change the signal from right to left at the point of no return
- ▶ Take a left lifesaver before exiting the roundabout

Instructor Tip

If in doubt on approach to the roundabout a decision to stop should be made on the grounds of safety.

KEEP IT ON THE BLACK STUFF

USE OF MOTORCYCLE STANDS

Using the stand correctly is an important aspect of riding a motorcycle and is covered in detail during motorcycle training. Care must be taken in respect of the road surface, road camber and always ensure that the stand is fully extended or retracted. Practice and not rushing will ensure the stand is located or stowed away correctly.

> **Instructor Tip**
> Once the side stand is down, give it a little kick forward to make sure it is fully locked.

During the Module 2 test, candidates will usually use the stand twice, once at the start of the test and again at the end. Be aware that candidates have failed the Module 2 test for dropping their bike when they thought the stand was securely in place when it wasn't.

If the motorcycle only has a main stand, sufficient practice must be given during training to ensure the candidate is properly prepared and is comfortable using it.

Key points to remember:

- Use the stand that is more familiar
- Stow stand away properly after mounting the bike
- Side stand must be fully down and forward before leaning the bike over
- For the test, it will be easier to use the side stand
- If on a camber leave the motorcycle in first gear

RESPONSE TO SIGNS

To pass the Module 2 Test requires a good understanding of the Highway Code along with all road signs and road markings that are commonly encountered. Candidates can improve their road safety with knowledge and training, allowing them to practice planning ahead to react to hazards.

The examiner will check the candidate's response to road signs, road markings and speed limits by assessing their forward vision and responses.

They will also check for appropriate responses to traffic lights, pedestrian crossings, road traffic controllers (e.g. police officers and school crossing patrols) and other aspects of the Highway Code.

Poor, unsafe or inappropriate response to signs can result in both minor or major faults being recorded. Module 2 candidates are advised to study the Highway Code, even if they have already passed the motorcycle theory test.

Key points to remember:

- ▶ Learn what all road signs mean
- ▶ Understand the different painted road markings
- ▶ Generally, more paint equals more danger
- ▶ Know what to do at traffic lights and pedestrian crossings
- ▶ Respond safely and in plenty of time

TRAFFIC LIGHTS

Test candidates are required to understand traffic lights, their sequence, how filter lights work, where lifesavers and rear observations should be used, how to deal with cycle lanes, how to deal with congested junctions and how to position correctly.

There may also be traffic light considerations that are specific to a local area. Traffic light skills for the chosen test area are best learned and practiced by booking lessons with a local professional motorcycle training school.

Examiners look for good observation and planning when approaching traffic lights. They will want to see good judgement, with anticipation of the lights changing and appropriate use of speed and gears to maintain safe progress through traffic light controlled junctions. This judgement includes rear observations on approach and avoiding stopping suddenly if the lights turn red because of poor forward vision and a lack of anticipation.

Key points to remember:

- Always look well ahead
- Anticipate the lights changing
- Use good rear observations at all times
- Position in the centre of the lane
- Stop behind the solid white line if lights are on red
- A lifesaver is often required when turning at traffic lights

Instructor Tip

The traffic light sequence is:-
red, red and amber, green, amber, red.

INDEPENDENT RIDE

The independent ride is usually explained at the start of the test, but not implemented until later. The independent ride takes about 10 minutes and involves riding solo without any further directions being given.

The purpose of the independent ride is for the examiner to assess a candidate's ability to ride safely whilst making their own decisions.

The Independent ride takes one of two forms:

1) The candidate will be asked to pull over and will be shown a simple map or diagram to explain a route consisting of three road directions. The candidate must then complete the route and find a safe place to pull over. This process is often repeated three times to complete a 10 minute independent ride.

2) An alternative involves following a series of road signs. The examiner might say, "please follow road signs to the town centre, until directed otherwise".

Preparation can be covered locally with a professional motorcycle training school, whose instructors will know the local test routes.

Whilst on test, if a candidate does not understand the instruction, they should ask for clarification. But if a test candidate gets lost or goes off route, it is unlikely to affect the test result and the examiner is responsible for returning them to the correct route.

Key points to remember:

▶ A wrong turn will not affect the test result
▶ The examiner will keep the candidate on course
▶ Independent ride only lasts 10 minutes
▶ Don't panic, relax and observe well ahead
▶ Don't worry if you take a wrong turn

KEEP IT ON THE BLACK STUFF

RETURNING TO THE TEST CENTRE

Back at the test centre the examiner will indicate where to park. There is still room for error so candidates must remain vigilant until the motorcycle is safely parked, on its stand and with the engine turned off.

The candidate will be invited into the test centre to debrief and will be offered the option of having their motorcycle instructor present. This is advisable as minor or major faults requiring further training needs can be communicated directly to the candidate with the instructor in listening.

The examiner uses a marking sheet to highlight any faults and will seek candidate understanding on these to assert any safety issues. The examiner will ensure their feedback and marking process is understood by the candidate during the debrief.

To pass the test a candidate must have no more than 10 rider faults (referred to as minors), plus no major faults, which would result in a fail.

The examiner will issue a pass certificate and if a plastic ID card licence is held, will keep the old licence and offer for the new entitlement to be added and a new licence sent by post from the DVLA at no cost to the candidate.

In the event of a failed attempt, 10 working days must pass before a retake is permitted.

Instructor Tip
The test isn't over until the bike is securely on its side stand and switched off.

FIRST TIME ON THE ROAD

Riding alone on a big bike for the first time can be daunting. New riders should plan short and local journeys, carry out motorcycle safety checks for every journey and wear protective clothing.

Riders must take responsibility, anticipate the actions of others, ride defensively and keep their headlight on at all times. They should wear high visibility clothing, with priority given to being seen versus looking fashionable.

Remember: engine on, lights on, ride on.

Inexperienced riders should think before every manoeuvre, junction and hazard, with good all round observations and lifesavers.

Care must be taken in rush hour traffic and reduced visibility. The weather must be considered, ensuring sufficient layers are worn to deal with the wet and cold. Rest and drink stops should be planned, with consideration of how fatigue and dehydration can affect rider safety.

New riders should be aware that brand new motorcycle clothing can be uncomfortable and can cause distractions. Gloves or boots that are too tight may feel sore.

Becoming skilled with a new motorcycle requires practice and patience, getting used to a bike's acceleration, braking and new controls is imperative. This all takes time and new riders should not see their motorcycle as a new toy but should treat it and the roads with respect.

KEEP IT ON THE BLACK STUFF

TAKE RESPONSIBILITY

The fact is that riders account for too many road traffic accidents. At Motorcycle Riders Hub we embrace a philosophy of rider responsibility and not delegating our safety to other road users.

Bikers should always question what they can do to take greater responsibility, increase visibility, enhance skills and anticipate the actions of other road users.

By accepting that our perceived ability seldom matches our actual ability, the importance of ongoing training is crystal clear.

> **Instructor Tip**
> Passing the test is only the start of the journey.

Basic motorcycle training is just a stepping stone and is to motorcycling what base camp is to Everest. To reach the summit requires an investment and determination to succeed with ongoing motorcycle raining and to improve.

Professional motorcycle training schools can advise on the Enhanced Rider Scheme (ERS), which is a Driver and Vehicle Standards Agency (DVSA) initiative, along with BikeSafe, which is a police sponsored hazard awareness scheme.

Further advanced qualifications can be achieved by taking The Royal Society for the Prevention of Accidents (RoSPA) and the Institute of Advanced Motorists (IAM) motorcycle test.

Take responsibility and make a commitment to ongoing advanced training and accept that as bikers, our safety is always in our own hands.

Keep it on the black stuff.

TAKE FURTHER TRAINING

Passing the Module 2 Test and gaining a full motorcycle licence might feel like the end of the training journey. In reality it is just the start of an incredibly fulfilling and challenging journey.

Bikers must take responsibility for their vulnerability and seek ongoing opportunities to increase their knowledge, ability and road safety.

One opportunity, and a natural progression from passing the Module 2 Test is the Motorcycle Riders Hub Advanced Course. This is a unique video based modular introduction to give a basic introduction to advanced riding.

The Motorcycle Riders Hub Advanced Course introduces new riders to the world of advanced riding, giving an in-depth tutorial on how to make small riding changes for huge results.

Stay safe, keep it on the black stuff and join the Motorcycle Riders Hub Academy, to start improving your riding to a new level.

> **Instructor Tip**
> Passing the test is only the beginning, and the first rung of the ladder. Don't leave progression to trial and error.

KEEP IT ON THE BLACK STUFF

Printed in Great Britain
by Amazon